FRED and ORBIT

HEADED SOON...TO THE MOON!

STEPHEN WHITE ILLUSTRATION
email: stref70@yahoo.co.uk   mobile: 07467202935

FRED and ORBIT

FRED AND ORBIT COPYRIGHT©STEPHEN WHITE 2025

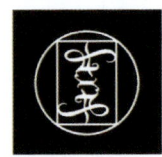

Orbit woke Fred, said, *"Get out of your bed!
Ted, it's six thirty three."* Fred said, *"Too early for me!
Five more minutes I feel are required!"*

Orb said, *"Sure that's okay, on an ORDINARY day!"*
And he shook the poor teddy, tried to shoogle him ready,
Fred got up, but complained of being tired.

"Today's a bit special," said Orb, "I built a vessel!"
And he unveiled a ship, that was fully equiped,
To take Orbit and Fred to the moon!

That robot told Fred, he'd got it into his head,
That the moon would be nice, for a while-hang the price!
So they blasted off round about noon.

As they sailed through the air,
Fred had not a care,
Or a hair, or much of a clue!

But that robot, he's smart,
He's as sharp as a dart,
Yes, he ALWAYS knows what to do.

The pair circled the world,
How they spun, how they burled,
And soon they were in outer space!

The moon was in sight,
Orb could see by its light,
A huge grin fixed on Fred Bear's smooth face!

"We're landing real soon,
On the face of the moon!"
Announced Orbit, "So hold on tight."

"What if we crashed,
And our spaceship got smashed?"
Worried Fred, "We'll be stuck there all night!"

But Orbit did good,
Landed just as you should,
In a crater, as wide as a mile.

Fred shouted for joy,
Quite loud for a toy,
Even Orb couldn't hold back a smile!

"We made it!" Fred screamed,
Or so it had seemed,
Orb confirmed when he checked all the data.

"Green to go," he agreed,
"We were bound to succeed,
I knew we'd get here sooner or later!"

Then they opened the door,
A hole in the floor!
And peered down on the lunar surface.

"You first?" proposed Fred,
And if truth were said,
Orb would swear that that Teddy was nervous!

"After you," Orb replied,
So Fred went, wide-eyed!
Said, "I'm not scared, I was just being polite!"

Fred's legs wobbled a bit,
As he stepped from the ship,
"From the cold," he would say, "Not the fright!"

*"So it's not made of cheese?
And it's cold!"* and Fred sneezed,
"And it's empty," he said, *"Nothing to do!"*

*Then Orbit stepped down,
Had a good look around,
Said, "It's just rocks, and a crater or two!"*

"Then, there's nothing up here?"
Fred said, "No atmosphere?
No water? No swingparks? No AIR?"

"'What did you assume,
Would be on the moon?"
Asked Orbit, "You silly old bear!"

"I thought parks, surely trees,
Maybe sharks, honey bees,"
Fred said, "You know Orb? Something like that!"

"There is moon dust and stars,
And you're closer to Mars!"
Explained Orbit, he knows where it's at!

Orbit just stood amazed,
With a look on his face,
That you won't see on many a robot.

"It's fantastic!" he said,
"I'm impressed little ted!"
Fred just didn't think it was so hot!

*"There's nothing around,
Not a smell, not a sound,
There's nothing but ground!"* complained Fred.

Things didn't improve,
When he started to move,
And his feet flew right over his head!

"There's less gravity here,"
Orb said, "Bear, do you hear?
There's a sixth here, of that on the earth!"

"So everything's light?"
Exclaimed Fred, "Out of sight!"
And went bouncing for all he was worth!

"It's not so bad here!"
Shouted Fred, with a cheer,
"All this bouncing is all well and good.

But tell me, good friend,
Upon whom I depend,
Where on moon will we find us some food?"

"Before we return,"
Said the robot, concerned,
"We must leave something to mark our adventure."

"I've forgotten the flag!"
Shrieked Fred, "What a drag,"
Orb, are there any ideas you could venture?"

Orbit had an idea,
To him it was clear,
And he had just the thing in his nose!

A little machine,
Very shiny and green,
What was it for, do you suppose?

"It's a hologram maker!"
Informed Orb-the big faker!
"It makes pictures that seem almost real."

"It looks good to me,"
Fred said, "But could it be,
That the people might notice, you feel?"

"They're too far off to see,"
Said Orb, "listen to me,"
But Fred was staring over Orb's shoulder.

He looked kind of scared,
Like he daren't of dared,
Saw something behind that big boulder!

What was the matter?
How Fred's teeth did chatter,
And his knees, they were knocking in tune!

More than slightly alarmed,
With googebumps on his arms,
Fred said, *"Are there people who live on the moon?"*

"Why, don't be absurd!
Can't believe what I've heard."
Said Orb, "Where do you get your ideas?"

Fred said, "Just turn around,
And I think you'll have found,
Enough data to share all my fears!"

And surely enough,
For a robot it's tough,
To admit that you're wrong...but it's true.

Time for pride had run out,
Without a shadow of doubt,
There was plenty of running to do!

And that's where it ends,
For our little toy friends,
But the ending is not really a bad thing.

His mother HAD called,
After all, all of this...ALL,
Was imagined! Imagine!! Imagined!!!

Printed in Great Britain
by Amazon